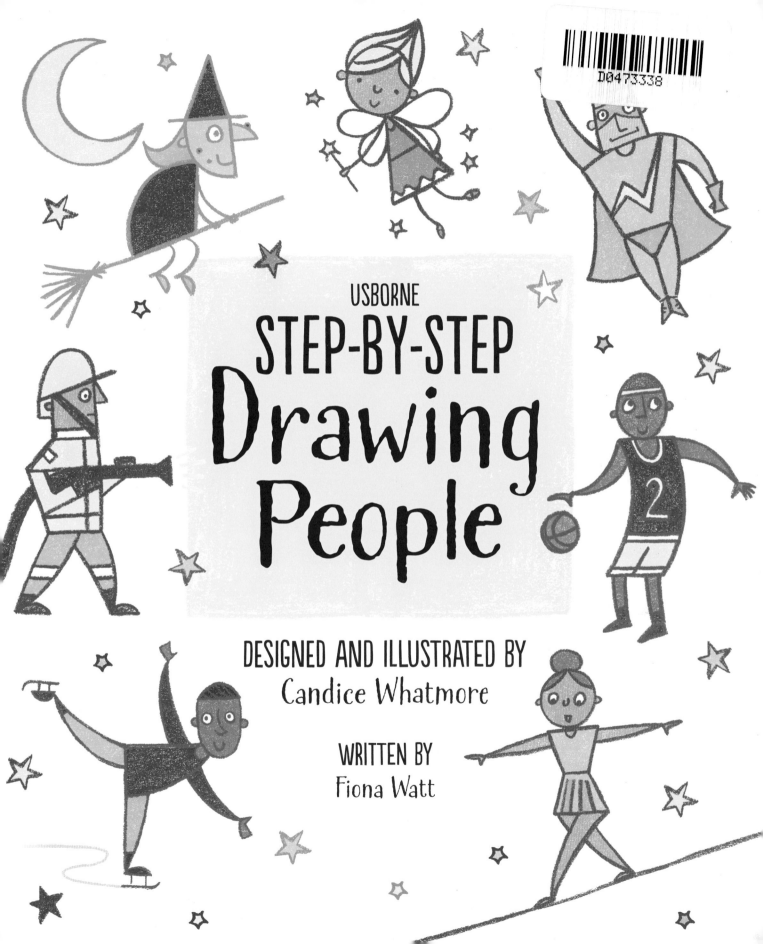

USBORNE
STEP-BY-STEP
Drawing
People

DESIGNED AND ILLUSTRATED BY
Candice Whatmore

WRITTEN BY
Fiona Watt

How to draw a superhero

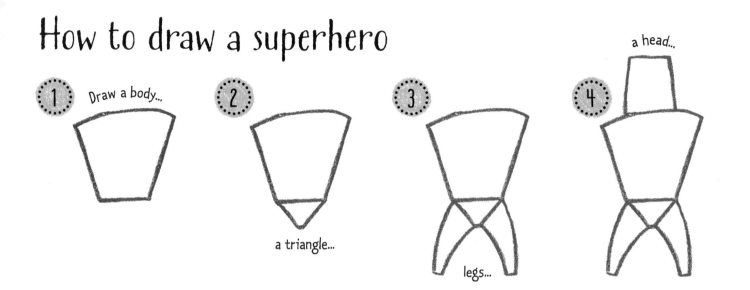

1. Draw a body...

2. a triangle...

3. legs...

4. a head...

Your turn...

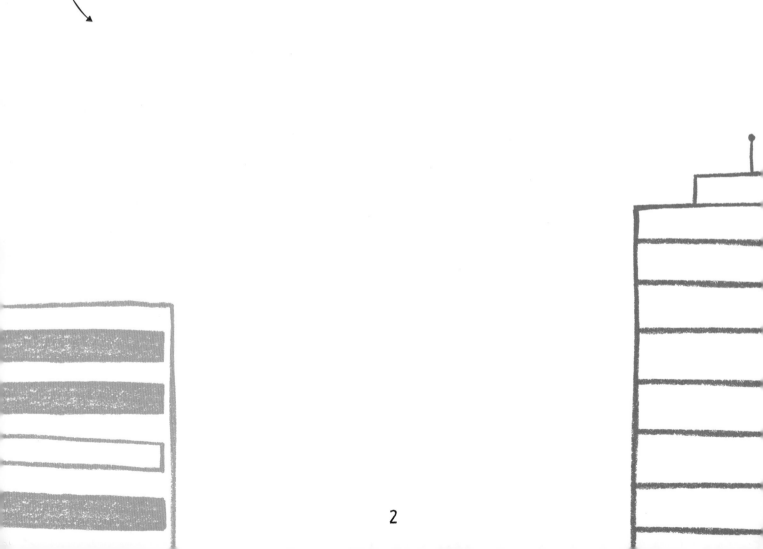

5

a face mask...

two arms...

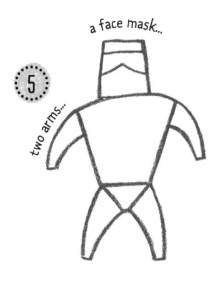

6

a neck...

gloves...

feet...

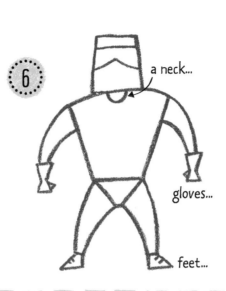

7

hair...

eyes, ears, a nose and a mouth...

and a cape.

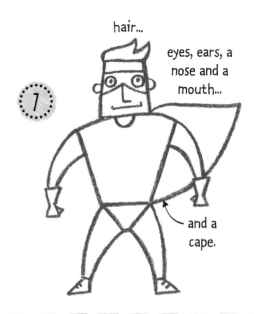

Try this...

To make a superhero fly, draw the body and head as before, then...

draw one arm up like this...

a logo...

legs like this...

and a cape.

How to draw an elf

1 Draw a square... a rectangle...

2 a hat... two legs...

3 hair... ears... a beard... a belt and buttons...

4 a bell... eyes, a nose and a mouth... arms and hands. Fill in the hair and his beard.

Your turn...

How to draw a fairy

1. Draw a circle...

2. a triangular body... a line...

3. two curved lines... another curve...

4. long hair... two arms... two legs...

Your turn...

5 strands of hair...

hands...

feet...

6 eyes, a nose, a mouth and ears...

wings...

frills...

7 magical stars...

and a wand.

How to draw Santa

1 Draw a half circle...

2 a beard...

3 a body...

4 a triangular hat... a triangle...

Your turn...

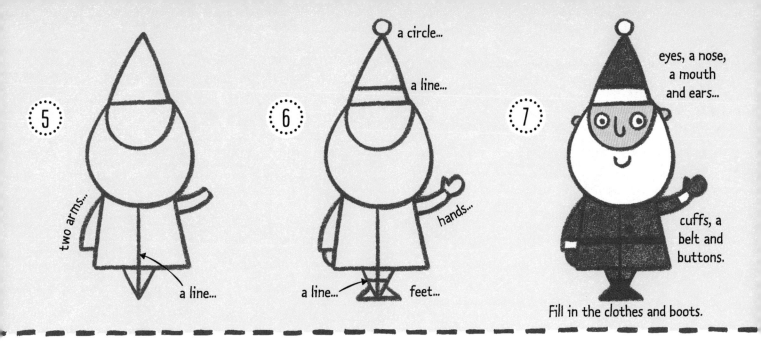

5 two arms... a line...

6 a circle... a line... hands... a line... feet...

7 eyes, a nose, a mouth and ears... cuffs, a belt and buttons. Fill in the clothes and boots.

How to draw a wizard

Your turn...

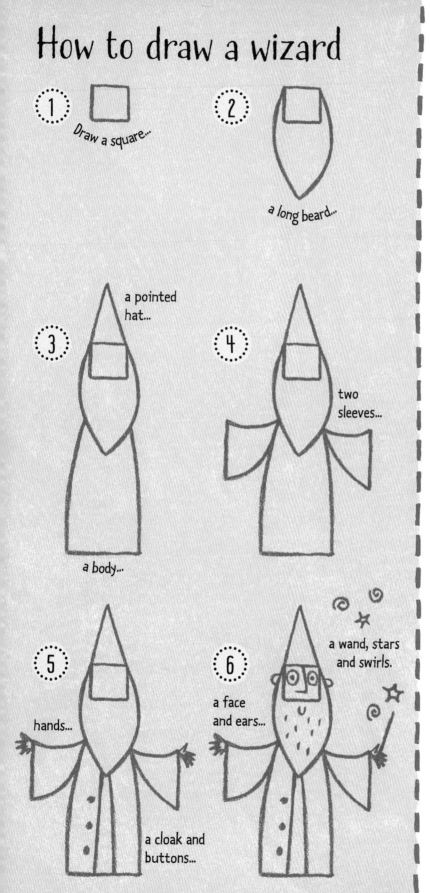

1 Draw a square...

2 a long beard...

3 a pointed hat...

a body...

4 two sleeves...

5 hands...

a cloak and buttons...

6 a face and ears...

a wand, stars and swirls.

How to draw a mummy

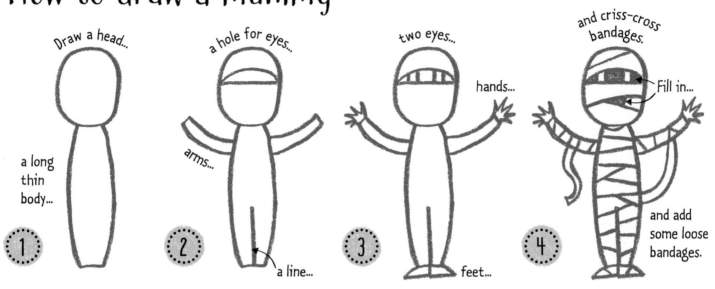

Draw a head...

a long thin body...

1

a hole for eyes...

arms...

a line...

2

two eyes...

hands...

feet...

3

and criss-cross bandages.

Fill in...

and add some loose bandages.

4

Your turn...

How to draw a witch

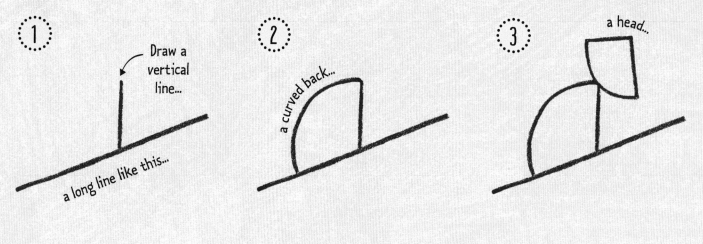

1 Draw a vertical line...

a long line like this...

2 a curved back...

3 a head...

Your turn...

4 a pointed hat...

two arms with hands...

5 a pointed nose...

hair...

two curved legs...

6 an eye, a mouth, and an ear...

a few warts...

a broom end...

and shoes.

Try this...

To draw a spooky witch silhouette, first draw a large yellow circle for the moon, then follow the steps above. Instead of adding a face, fill in the whole shape so that it looks like this:

How to draw a zombie

Your turn...

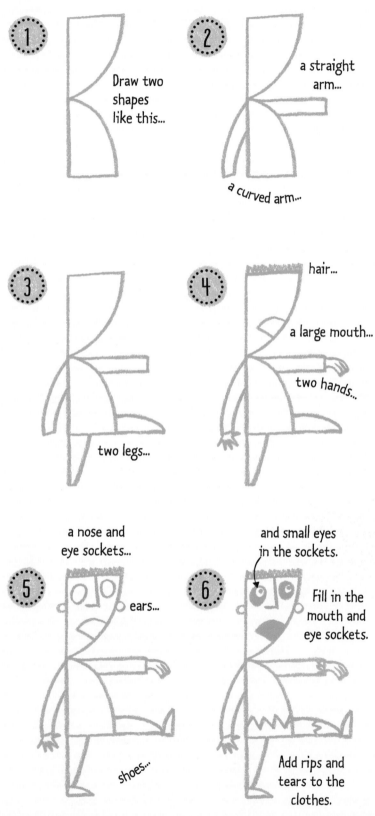

1 Draw two shapes like this...

2 a straight arm...

a curved arm...

3 two legs...

4 hair...

a large mouth...

two hands...

5 a nose and eye sockets...

ears...

shoes...

6 and small eyes in the sockets.

Fill in the mouth and eye sockets.

Add rips and tears to the clothes.

16

How to draw a mermaid

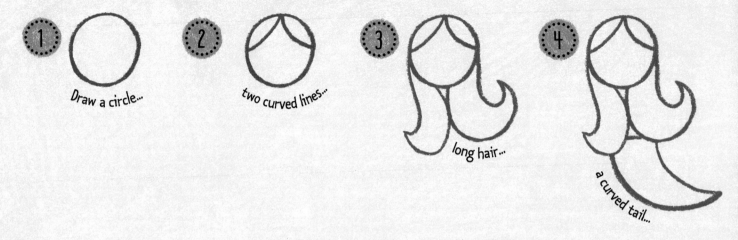

1 Draw a circle...

2 two curved lines...

3 long hair...

4 a curved tail...

Your turn...

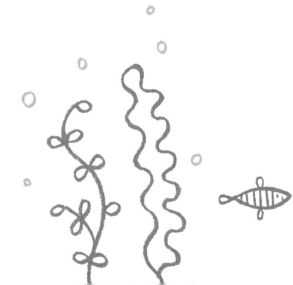

5 two arms...

6 lines in the hair...

hands...

two fins...

7 eyes, a nose, and a mouth.

Add bubbles and fish...

and scales.

19

How to draw a pirate captain

 1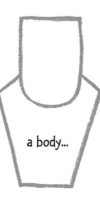

Draw a head...

2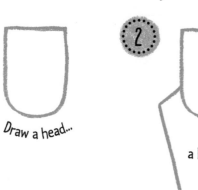

a body...

3

a curve...

two lines...

4

a pirate hat...

arms...

Your turn...

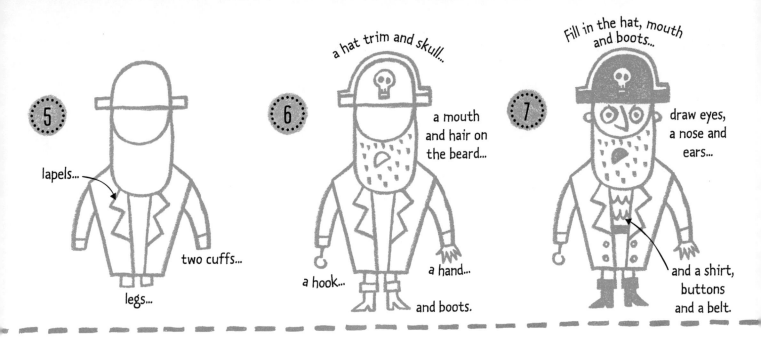

5 lapels...

two cuffs...

legs...

6 a hat trim and skull...

a mouth and hair on the beard...

a hook...

a hand...

and boots.

7 Fill in the hat, mouth and boots...

draw eyes, a nose and ears...

and a shirt, buttons and a belt.

21

How to draw a Roman

Your turn...

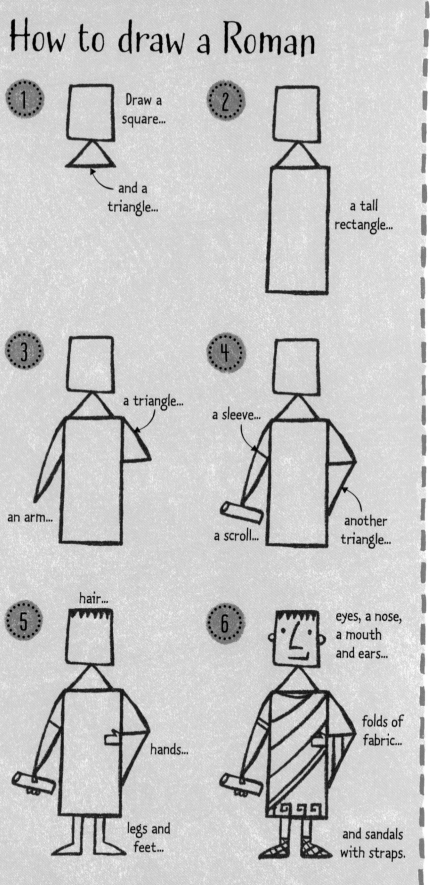

1 Draw a square... and a triangle...

2 a tall rectangle...

3 a triangle... an arm...

4 a sleeve... a scroll... another triangle...

5 hair... hands... legs and feet...

6 eyes, a nose, a mouth and ears... folds of fabric... and sandals with straps.

How to draw a Viking

1. Draw a rectangle...

2. a circle... and a smaller circle inside...

3. a body... shoulders...

4. a helmet... an arm... a rectangle...

Your turn...

24

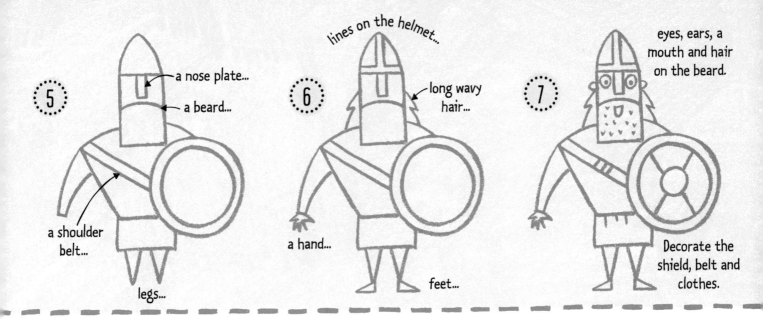

5

a nose plate...

a beard...

a shoulder belt...

legs...

6

lines on the helmet...

long wavy hair...

a hand...

feet...

7

eyes, ears, a mouth and hair on the beard.

Decorate the shield, belt and clothes.

25

How to draw a circus ringmaster

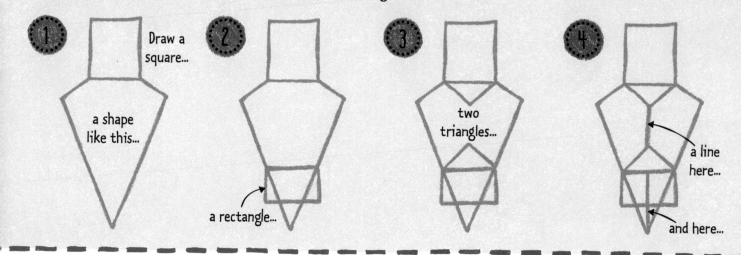

1 Draw a square... a shape like this...

2 a rectangle...

3 two triangles...

4 a line here... and here...

Your turn...

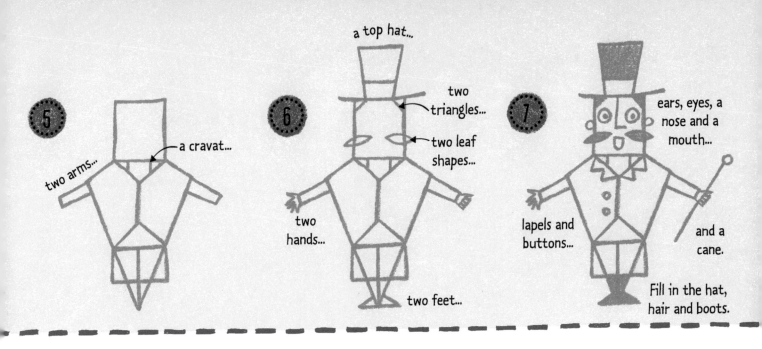

5 two arms... a cravat...

6 a top hat... two triangles... two leaf shapes... two hands... two feet...

7 ears, eyes, a nose and a mouth... lapels and buttons... and a cane. Fill in the hat, hair and boots.

How to draw a clown

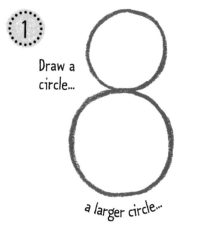

1 Draw a circle...

a larger circle...

2 an X across the body...

3 big curly hair...

arms...

legs...

Your turn...

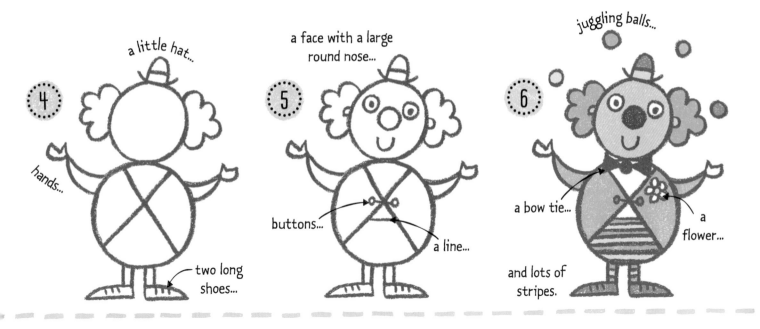

④ a little hat...

hands...

two long shoes...

⑤ a face with a large round nose...

buttons...

a line...

⑥ juggling balls...

a bow tie...

a flower...

and lots of stripes.

Try this...

Draw your clown with a different face, body shape or clothes. Here are some ideas. You could copy these or invent your own.

How to draw a circus strongman

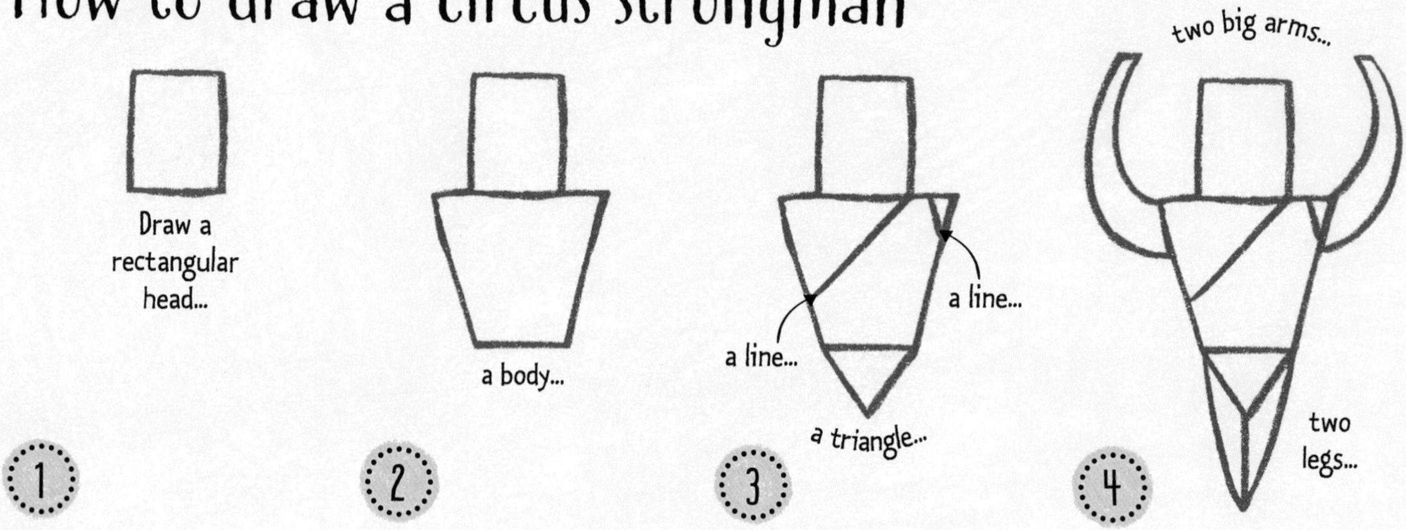

Draw a
rectangular
head...

a body...

a line...

a line...

a triangle...

two big arms...

two
legs...

1

2

3

4

Your turn...

30

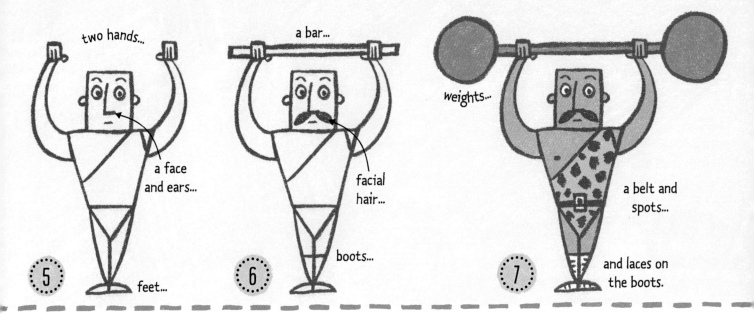

two hands...

a face
and ears...

feet...

5

a bar...

facial
hair...

boots...

6

weights...

a belt and
spots...

and laces on
the boots.

7

31

How to draw a tightrope walker

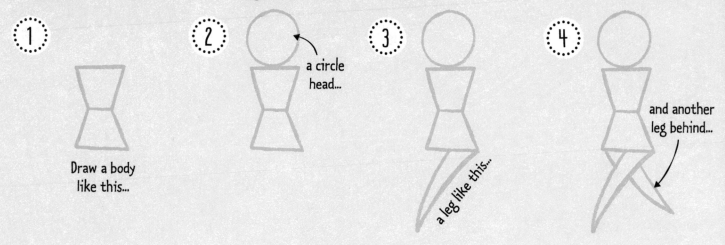

1. Draw a body like this...

2. a circle head...

3. a leg like this...

4. and another leg behind...

Your turn...

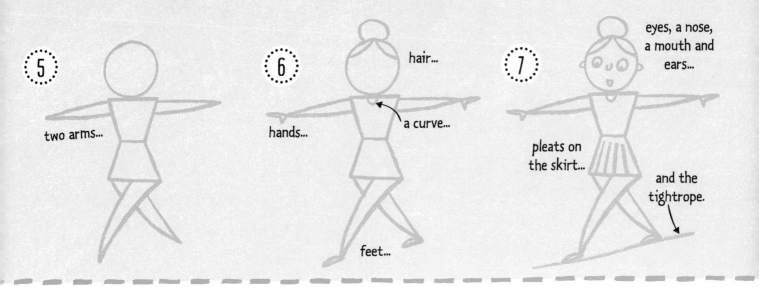

5 two arms...

6 hair... hands... a curve... feet...

7 eyes, a nose, a mouth and ears... pleats on the skirt... and the tightrope.

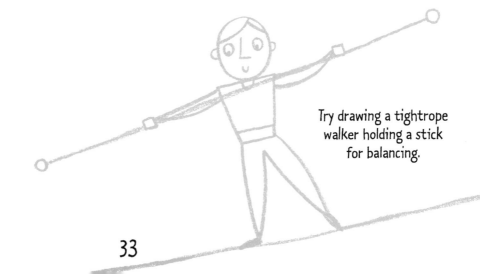

Try drawing a tightrope walker holding a stick for balancing.

How to draw a tourist

 Draw a head...

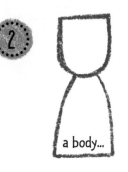 a body...

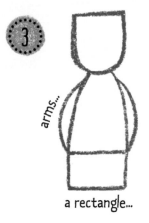 arms... a rectangle...

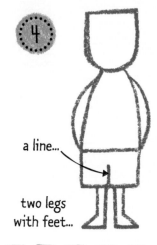 a line... two legs with feet...

Your turn...

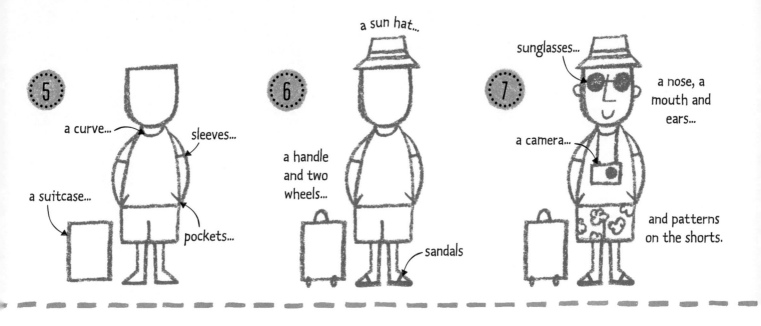

5 a curve... sleeves... a suitcase... pockets...

6 a sun hat... a handle and two wheels... sandals

7 sunglasses... a nose, a mouth and ears... a camera... and patterns on the shorts.

Draw more tourists and lots of suitcases.

How to draw a cowboy

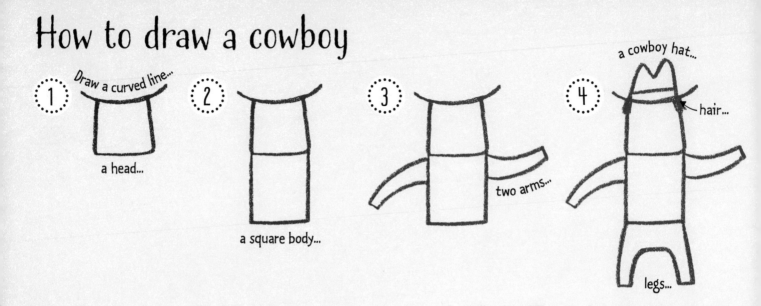

1 Draw a curved line...
a head...

2 a square body...

3 two arms...

4 a cowboy hat...
hair...
legs...

Your turn...

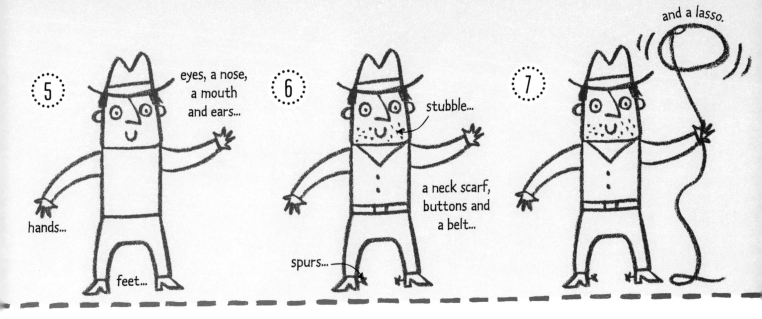

5 eyes, a nose, a mouth and ears...

hands...

feet...

6 stubble...

a neck scarf, buttons and a belt...

spurs...

7 and a lasso.

How to draw a cowgirl

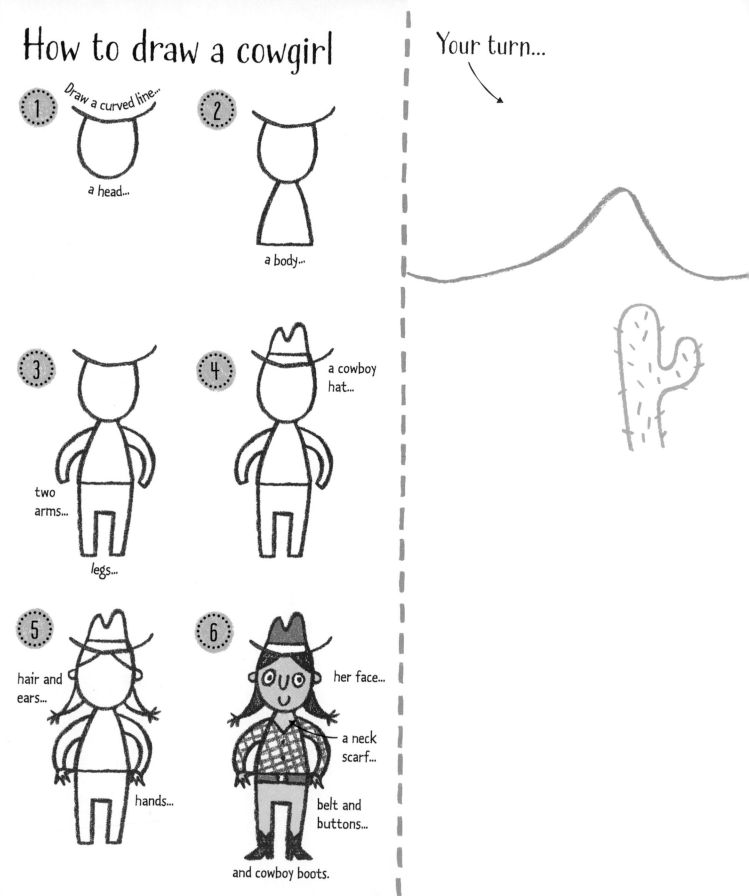

1 Draw a curved line...
a head...

2 a body...

3 two arms...
legs...

4 a cowboy hat...

5 hair and ears...
hands...

6 her face...
a neck scarf...
belt and buttons...
and cowboy boots.

38

How to draw a kokeshi doll

Draw a circle...

1

a body...

2

two sleeves...

3

a bun...

hair...

and a hand.

4

Fill in the hair...

draw a face and ears...

a kimono...

and two feet.

5

Your turn...

40

How to draw an explorer

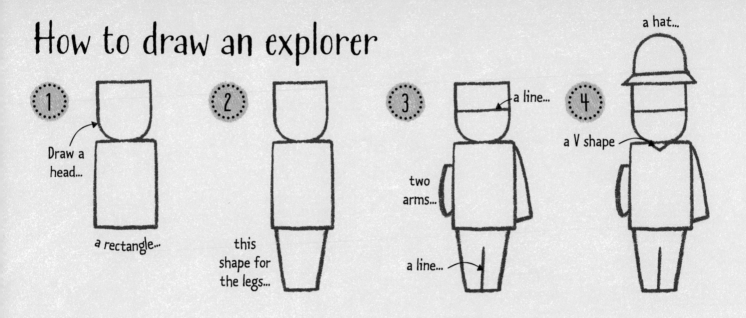

1 Draw a head... a rectangle...

2 this shape for the legs...

3 a line... two arms... a line...

4 a hat... a V shape a line...

Your turn...

Draw large leaves around your explorer – he'll look like he's in the jungle.

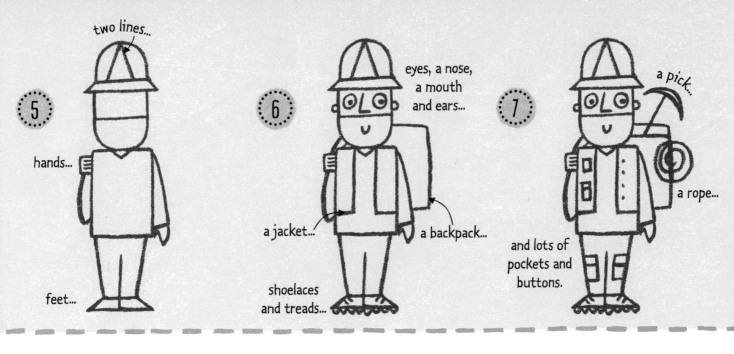

5 two lines...

hands...

feet...

6 eyes, a nose, a mouth and ears...

a jacket...

a backpack...

shoelaces and treads...

7 a pick...

a rope...

and lots of pockets and buttons.

Try this...

To draw an Arctic explorer, add boots, a warm jacket and a fur-lined hood instead.

fur hood

warm jacket

snow boots

How to draw a tap dancer

1 Draw a head...

2 a body...

3 two shapes like this...

4 arms... legs...

- -

Your turn...

5 a top hat...
a bow tie...
a jacket tail...

6 hands...
buttons...
shoes and laces...

7 eyes, a nose, a mouth and ears...
and a cane.
Fill in the suit and hat.
TAP

45

How to draw a ballerina

Your turn...

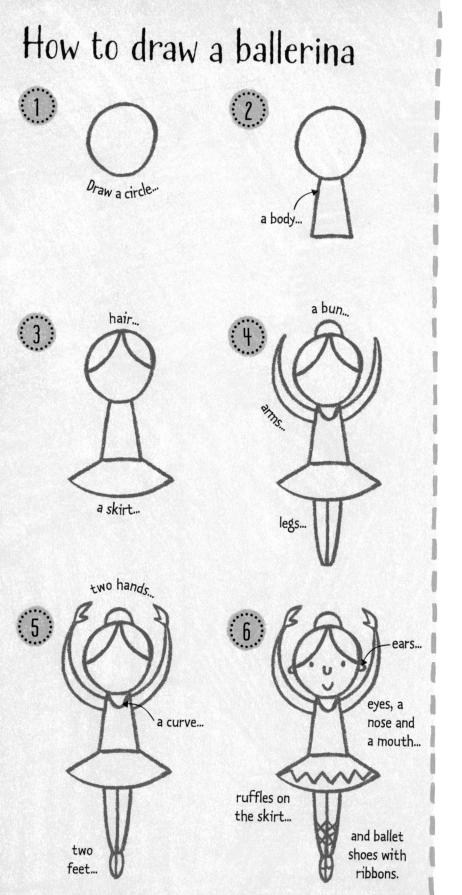

1 Draw a circle...

2 a body...

3 hair...
   a skirt...

4 a bun...
   arms...
   legs...

5 two hands...
   a curve...
   two feet...

6 ears...
   eyes, a nose and a mouth...
   ruffles on the skirt...
   and ballet shoes with ribbons.

46

Try this...

Draw your ballerina in different positions by altering the legs, arms or both. Here are some ideas. You could copy these or try your own.

arms up

legs crossed

arms down

legs crossed, feet flat

arm down   arm up

balanced on one leg

How to draw an ice skater

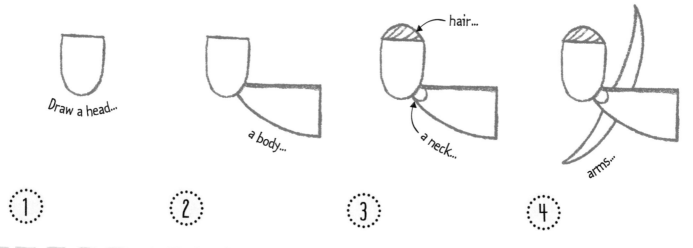

Draw a head...

a body...

hair...

a neck...

arms...

① ② ③ ④

Your turn...

48

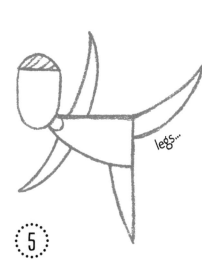

legs...

5

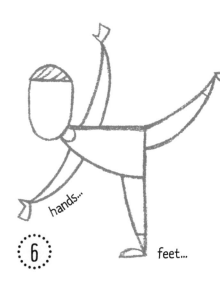

hands...

feet...

6

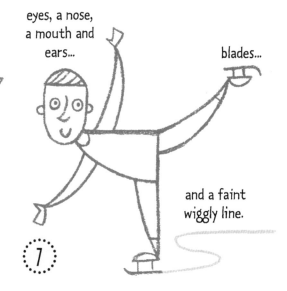

eyes, a nose, a mouth and ears...

blades...

and a faint wiggly line.

7

How to draw a movie star

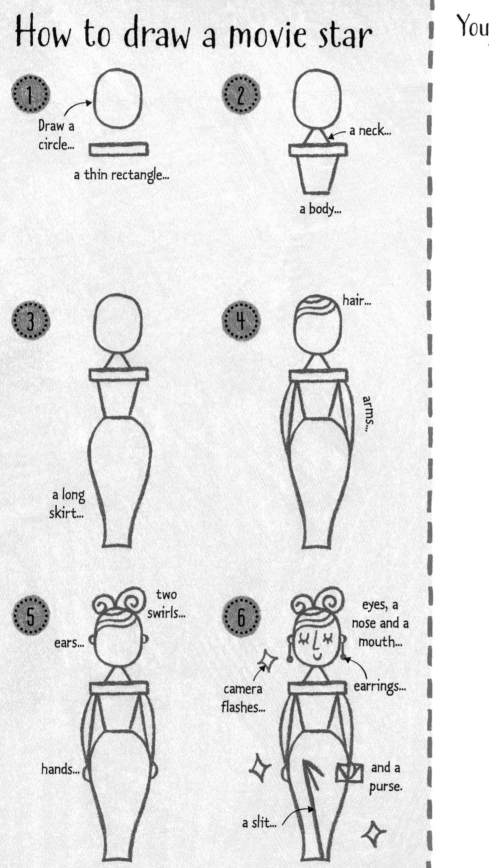

1 Draw a circle... a thin rectangle...

2 a neck... a body...

3 a long skirt...

4 hair... arms...

5 two swirls... ears... hands...

6 eyes, a nose and a mouth... earrings... camera flashes... a slit... and a purse.

Your turn...

How to draw a singer

Your turn...

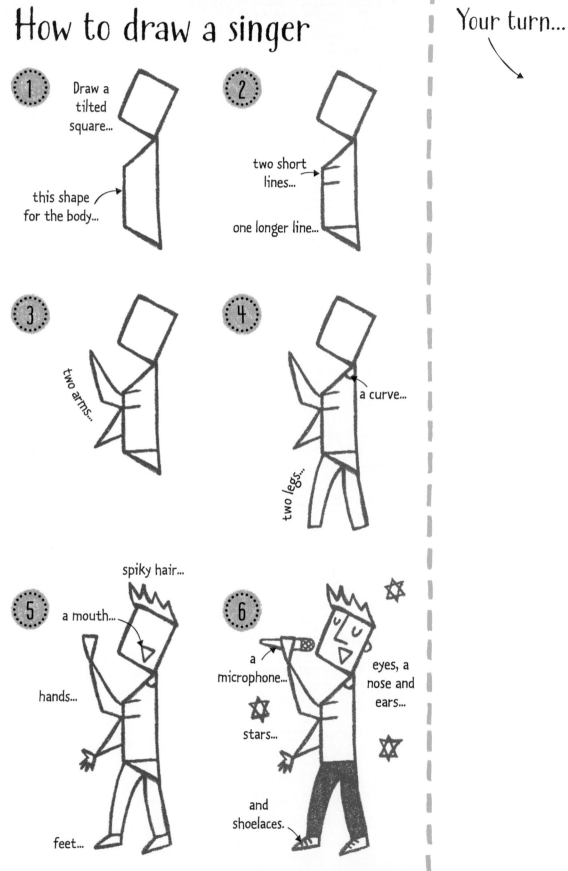

1 Draw a tilted square...

this shape for the body...

2 two short lines...

one longer line...

3 two arms...

4 a curve...

two legs...

5 spiky hair...

a mouth...

hands...

feet...

6 a microphone...

eyes, a nose and ears...

stars...

and shoelaces.

52

How to draw a king

1 Draw a head...

2 a big beard...

3 a body...

4 a crown...

Your turn...

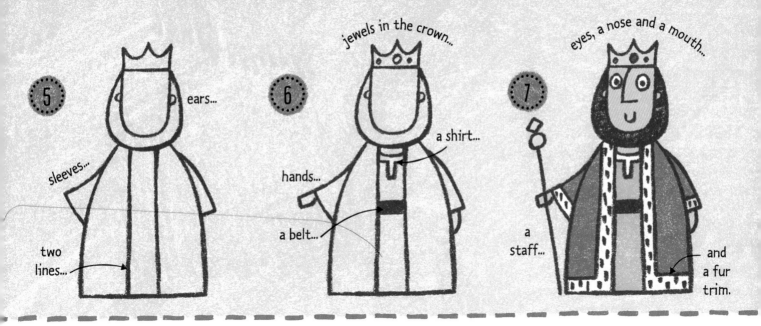

5 ears...

sleeves...

two lines...

6 jewels in the crown...

hands...

a shirt...

a belt...

7 eyes, a nose and a mouth...

a staff...

and a fur trim.

How to draw a queen

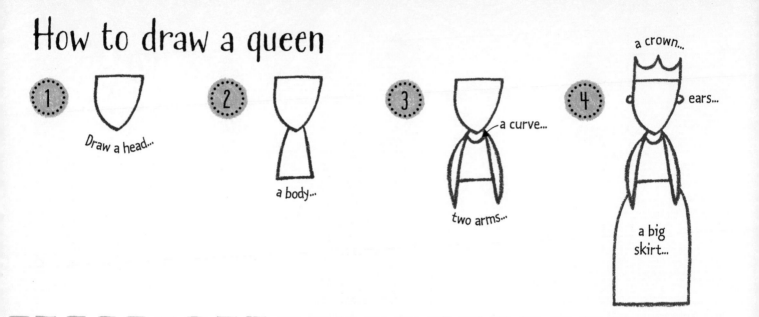

1 Draw a head...

2 a body...

3 a curve... two arms...

4 a crown... ears... a big skirt...

Your turn...

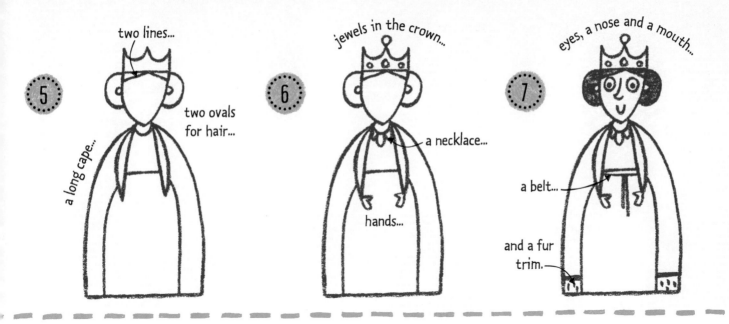

5 two lines...

two ovals for hair...

a long cape...

6 jewels in the crown...

a necklace...

hands...

7 eyes, a nose and a mouth...

a belt...

and a fur trim.

How to draw a guardsman

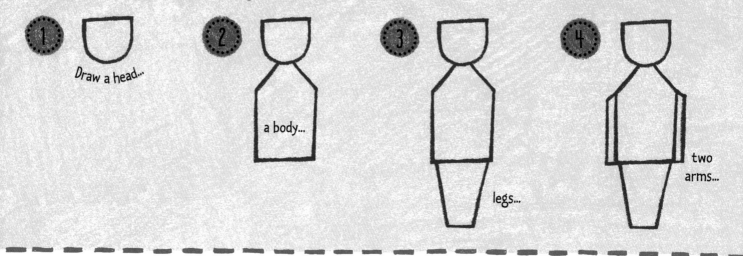

1 Draw a head...

2 a body...

3 legs...

4 two arms...

Your turn...

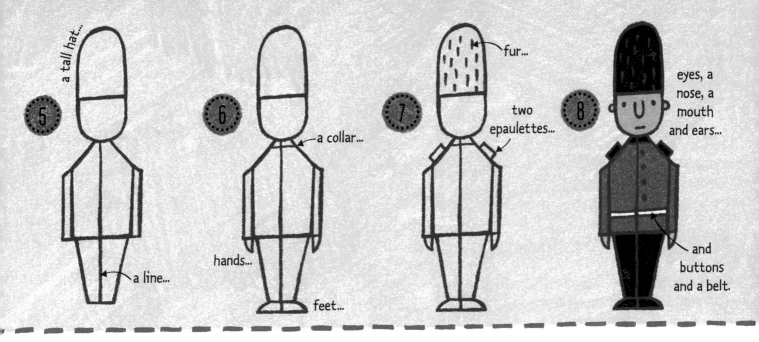

5 a tall hat... a line...

6 a collar... hands... feet...

7 fur... two epaulettes...

8 eyes, a nose, a mouth and ears... and buttons and a belt.

How to draw a little boy

1 Draw a circle...

2 a body...

3 a line for hair... shorts...

4 a neck... arms... legs...

5 strands of hair... two sleeves... feet...

6 eyes, ears, a nose, and a mouth.

Your turn...

How to draw a little girl

1. Draw a circle...

2. a body...

3. a neck...
   a line for a skirt...

4. two curved lines...
   two arms...
   two legs...

5. pigtails...
   hands...
   feet...

6. eyes, ears, a nose, and a mouth...
   and pleats.

Your turn...

How to draw an old man

Your turn...

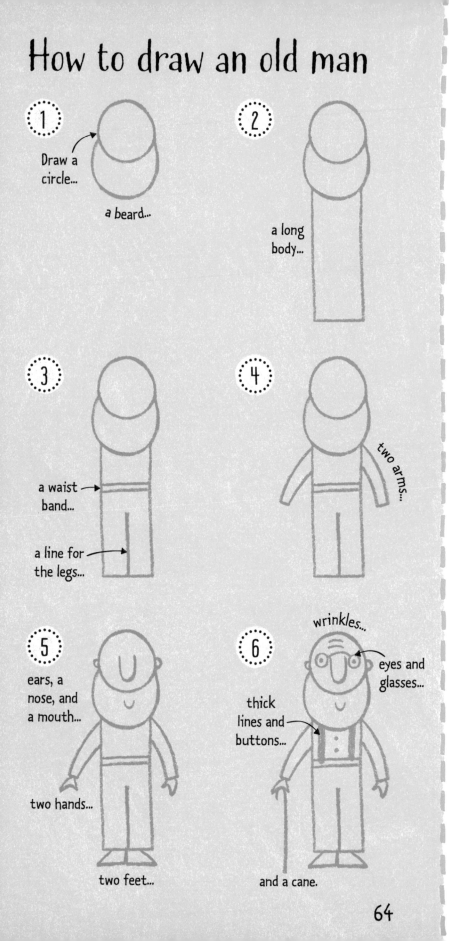

1 Draw a circle...

a beard...

2 a long body...

3 a waist band...

a line for the legs...

4 two arms...

5 ears, a nose, and a mouth...

two hands...

two feet...

6 wrinkles...

eyes and glasses...

thick lines and buttons...

and a cane.

How to draw an old lady

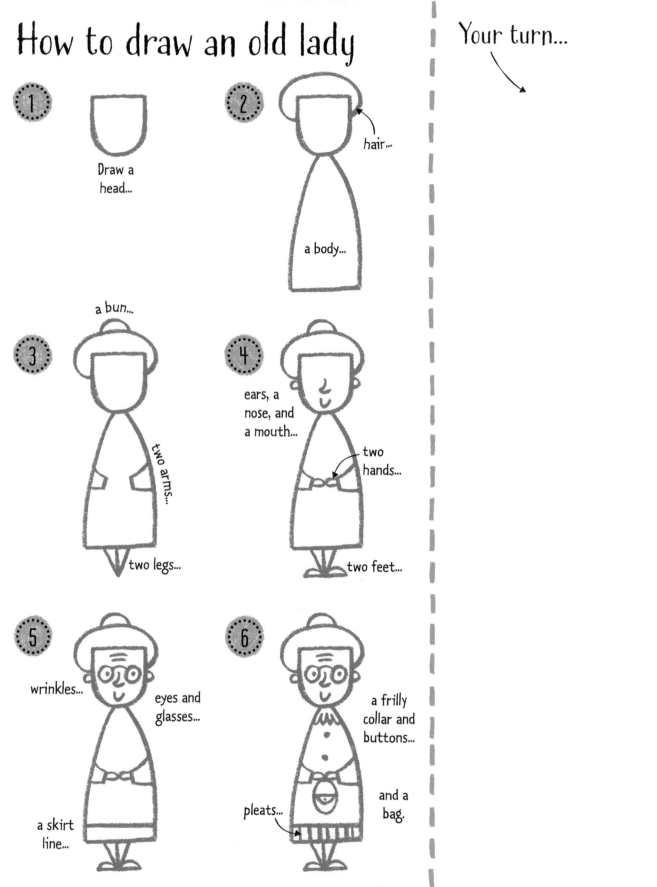

1. Draw a head...

2. hair... a body...

3. a bun... two arms... two legs...

4. ears, a nose, and a mouth... two hands... two feet...

5. wrinkles... eyes and glasses... a skirt line...

6. a frilly collar and buttons... pleats... and a bag.

How to draw a basketball player

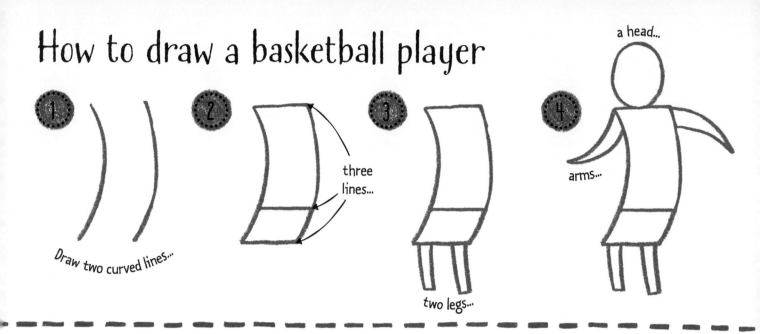

1. Draw two curved lines...

2. three lines...

3. two legs...

4. a head...

arms...

Your turn...

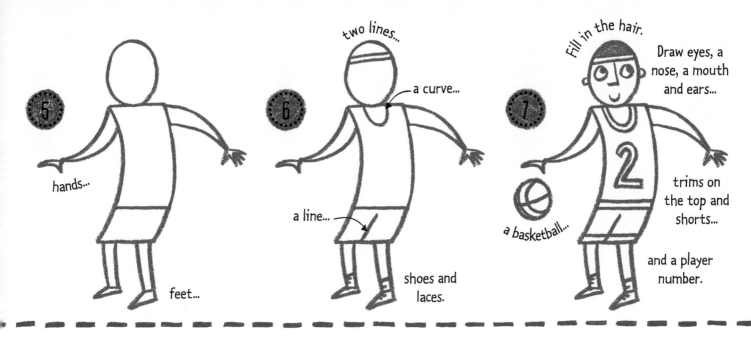

5 hands... feet...

6 two lines... a curve... a line... shoes and laces.

7 Fill in the hair. Draw eyes, a nose, a mouth and ears... trims on the top and shorts... and a player number. a basketball...

Try this...

Change the position of the legs to make your player run. Add some movement lines beneath the ball.

69

How to draw a bride

 1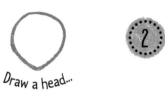

Draw a head...

2

a body...

3

a bunch of
flowers...

4

the top
of a
dress...

two
arms...

two hands...

- -

Your turn...

70

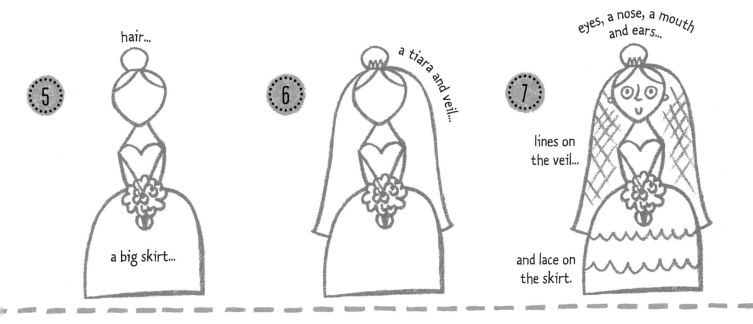

5 hair...

a big skirt...

6 a tiara and veil...

7 eyes, a nose, a mouth and ears...

lines on the veil...

and lace on the skirt.

How to draw a spy

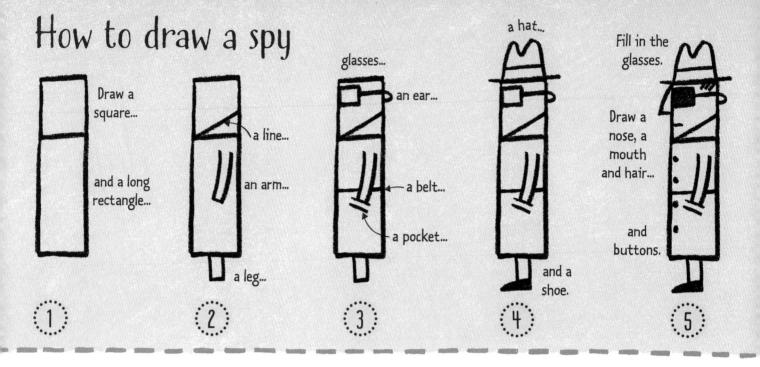

Draw a square...

and a long rectangle...

①

a line...

an arm...

a leg...

②

glasses...

an ear...

a belt...

a pocket...

③

a hat...

and a shoe.

④

Fill in the glasses.

Draw a nose, a mouth and hair...

and buttons.

⑤

Your turn...

This spy is handing over
his secret briefcase.
Draw more spies and
briefcases in a park.

How to draw a racing jockey

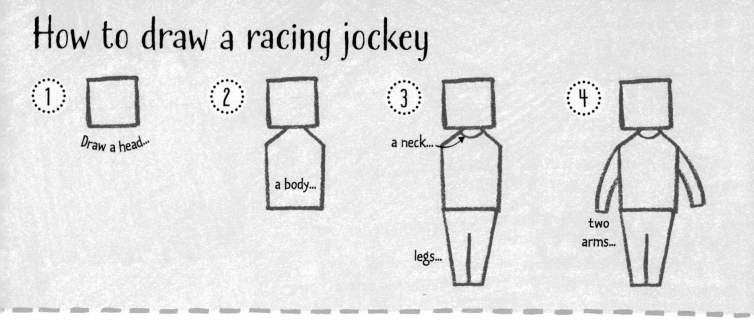

1 Draw a head...

2 a body...

3 a neck... legs...

4 two arms...

Your turn...

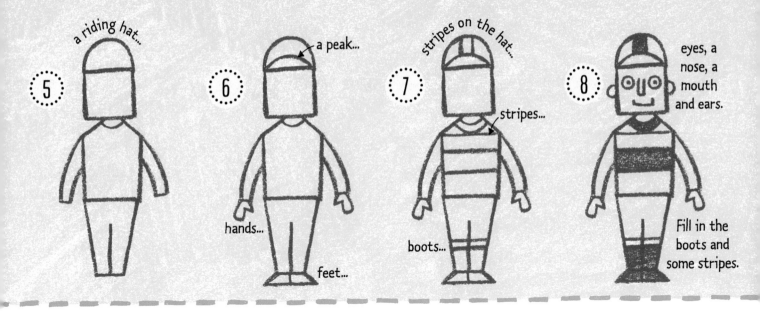

5 a riding hat...

6 a peak... hands... feet...

7 stripes on the hat... stripes... boots...

8 eyes, a nose, a mouth and ears.

Fill in the boots and some stripes.

How to draw a horse rider

1 Draw a head...

2 a body... a V shape...

3 jacket tails...

4 a riding hat... a shape for the legs...

Your turn...

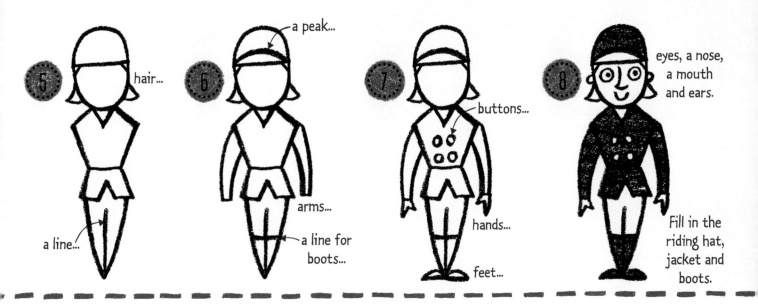

5 hair...

a line...

6 a peak...

arms...

a line for boots...

7 buttons...

hands...

feet...

8 eyes, a nose, a mouth and ears.

Fill in the riding hat, jacket and boots.

How to draw a builder

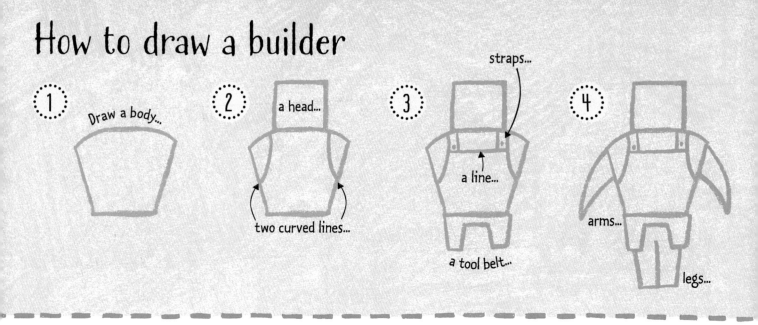

1. Draw a body...

2. a head...
   two curved lines...

3. straps...
   a line...
   a tool belt...

4. arms...
   legs...

Your turn...

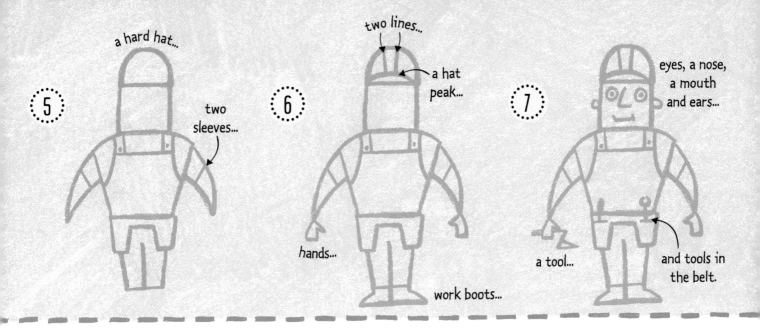

5 a hard hat...

two sleeves...

6 two lines...

a hat peak...

hands...

work boots...

7 eyes, a nose, a mouth and ears...

a tool...

and tools in the belt.

How to draw a doctor

Your turn...

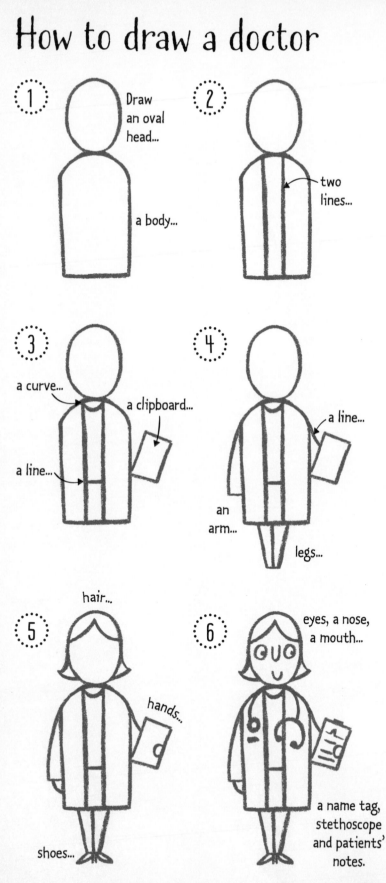

1. Draw an oval head... a body...

2. two lines...

3. a curve... a clipboard... a line...

4. a line... an arm... legs...

5. hair... hands... shoes...

6. eyes, a nose, a mouth... a name tag, stethoscope and patients' notes.

How to draw a nurse

Your turn...

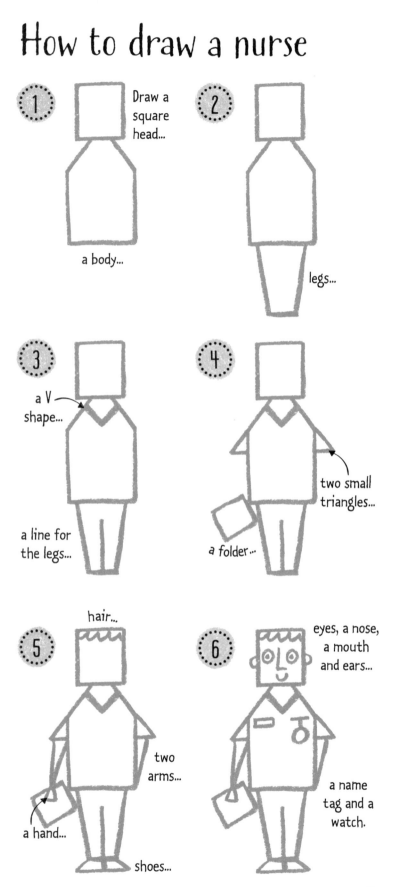

1 Draw a square head...

a body...

2 legs...

3 a V shape...

a line for the legs...

4 two small triangles...

a folder...

5 hair...

two arms...

a hand...

shoes...

6 eyes, a nose, a mouth and ears...

a name tag and a watch.

82

How to draw a firefighter

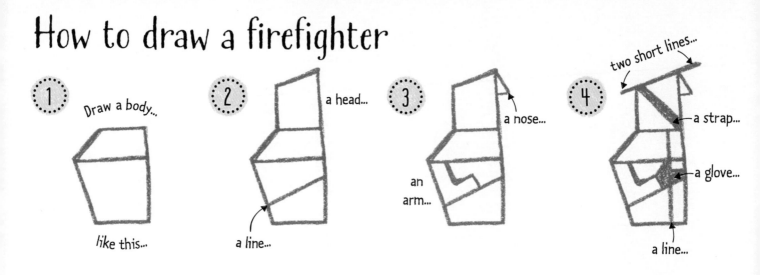

1 Draw a body...

like this...

2 a head...

a line...

3 a nose...

an arm...

4 two short lines...

a strap...

a glove...

a line...

Your turn...

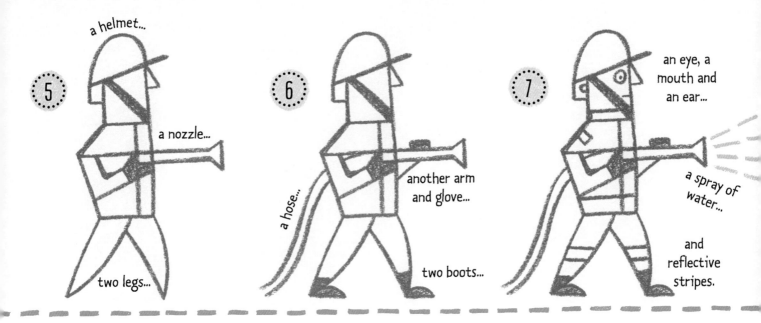

5 a helmet...

a nozzle...

two legs...

6 a hose...

another arm and glove...

two boots...

7 an eye, a mouth and an ear...

a spray of water...

and reflective stripes.

How to draw a waiter

1 Draw a head...

2 a body...

3 a curve and three lines...

4 legs...

Your turn...

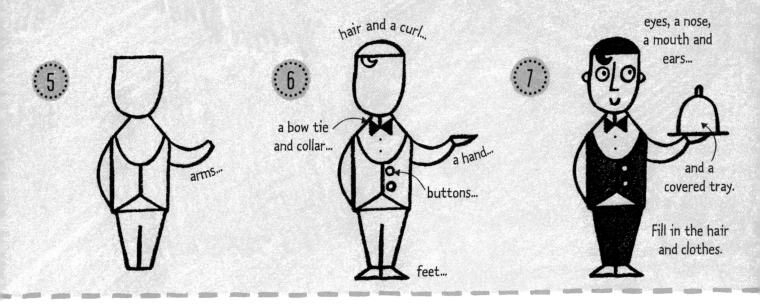

5
arms...

6
hair and a curl...
a bow tie and collar...
a hand...
buttons...
feet...

7
eyes, a nose, a mouth and ears...
and a covered tray.

Fill in the hair and clothes.

How to draw a chef

Your turn...

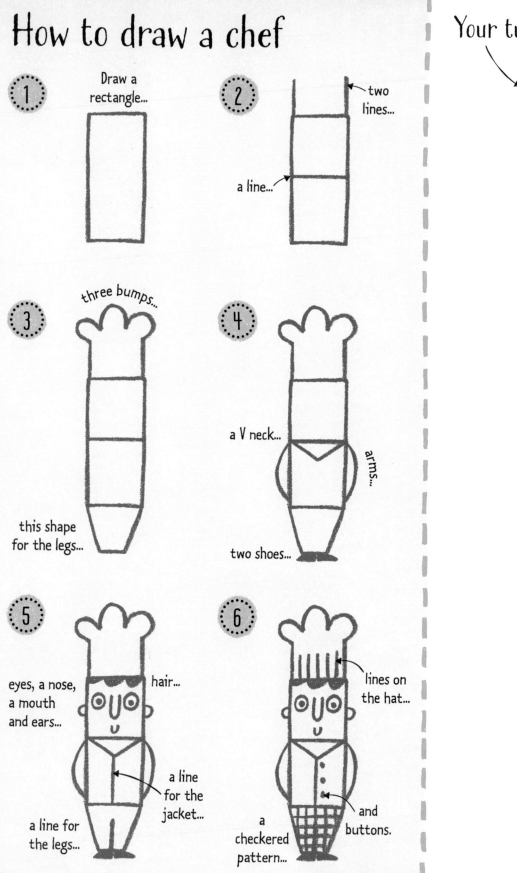

1 Draw a rectangle...

2 two lines... a line...

3 three bumps... this shape for the legs...

4 a V neck... arms... two shoes...

5 eyes, a nose, a mouth and ears... hair... a line for the jacket... a line for the legs...

6 lines on the hat... a checkered pattern... and buttons.

88

How to draw faces

smiley   surprised   happy   sad   angry

tired   excited   upset   asleep   content

Your turn... Draw different expressions on these heads, then draw some of your own...

Add hair...

shaved   curly   straight   long   short   pigtails

and accessories

glasses   eyebrows   beard   winter hat   cowboy hat   straw hat

Poses and gestures

walking

running

sitting

jumping

lifting

creeping

pushing

pulling

dancing

exercising

cheering

angry

thinking

puzzled

sad

"oh no!"

Create a character

1 Choose a pose or gesture or create your own.

2 Choose an expression (see page 90).

3 Put the two together.

4 Then, draw your character with clothes and hair.

Your turn...

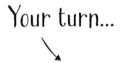

Create a scene

Fill this page with characters you might see at a party where everyone has come in a costume.

Aunt Anabella

Draw people in the picture frames,
then give them a name.

With thanks to Keith Furnival

First published in 2014 by Usborne Publishing Ltd., Usborne House, 83-85 Saffron Hill, London EC1N 8RT, England.
www.usborne.com © 2014 Usborne Publishing Ltd. The name Usborne and the devices 🎈 🎈 are Trade Marks of Usborne Publishing Ltd.